RIVERSIDE CHRISTIAN SCHOOL
3532 Monroe St.
Riverside, CA. 92504

Vincent
VAN GOGH

TELL ME ABOUT

Vincent
VAN GOGH

by John Malam

Carolrhoda Books, Inc. / Minneapolis

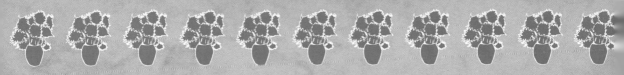

Carolrhoda Books, Inc., c/o The Lerner Publishing Group
241 First Avenue North, Minneapolis, Minnesota 55401 U.S.A.
Website address: www.lernerbooks.com

Library of Congress Cataloging-in-Publication Data

Malam, John.
  Vincent van Gogh / by John Malam.
    p. cm. — (Tell me about)·
  Includes index.
  Summary: Briefly examines the life of the renowned Dutch painter and
traces the development of his art.
  ISBN 1–57505–249–0 (alk. paper)
  1. Gogh, Vincent van, 1853–1890—Juvenile literature. 2. Painters—
Netherlands—Biography—Juvenile literature. [1. Gogh, Vincent van,
1853–1890. 2. Painters.] I. Title. II. Series: Tell me about (Minneapolis,
Minn.)
ND653.G7M28 1998
759.9492–dc21   97–8066

Printed by Graficas Reunidas SA, Spain
Bound in the United States of America
1 2 3 4 5 6 – OS – 03 02 01 00 99 98

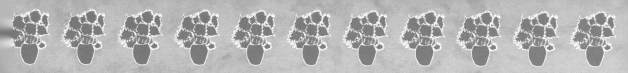

Vincent van Gogh was an artist. He was born in the Netherlands in 1853. He painted most of his pictures in the last ten years of his short life. It was only after he died that people realized what a great artist he really was. This is his story.

Vincent painted this picture of himself when he was thirty-five years old.

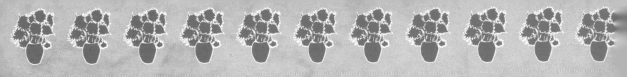

Vincent grew up in the Dutch village of Groot-Zundert. He had three sisters and two brothers. Vincent was the oldest. His father, Theodorus, was a minister. As a small boy, Vincent liked to watch his mother, Anna, draw. He began to draw some pictures of his own. They were very good.

The Netherlands is a flat country with many canals.

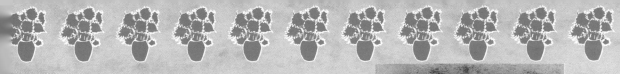

Vincent was not a happy child. People said he was rude and bad tempered. The little boy with red hair and freckles hardly ever smiled. He usually looked very serious.

Vincent when he was thirteen years old

When Vincent was older, he often drew people working in the fields.

Vincent's parents worried about their unhappy son. When he was sixteen, they sent him to work for his uncle. Uncle Cent was an art dealer. He bought and sold paintings. Vincent liked his uncle and enjoyed studying the paintings in his gallery.

Vincent called his uncle "Cent," which was short for Vincent.

Vincent worked in Paris in 1874.

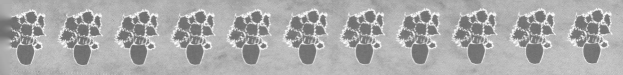

Vincent did well at his job and learned a lot about art. His uncle sent him to work in England and then in France so he could learn even more.

When Vincent was twenty-three years old, he left his job. He was unhappy again and had lost interest in his work.

For a time, he taught at a school in Ramsgate, a town on the southeast coast of England.

The square in Ramsgate where Vincent lived in 1876

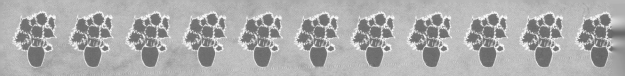

Before long, Vincent decided he wanted to work for the church, like his father. Vincent went to Belgium to be a minister. He worked in a poor region where there were many coal mines. He gave away all his best clothes to the people he met. He wore ragged clothes and cared for the sick.

Vincent worked hard, but he soon discovered that a minister's life was not right for him, either.

Vincent drew this picture in Belgium.

He had started drawing again, as he had when he was a child. He wondered if he could become an artist.

Vincent had always been close to his younger brother Theo. Theo had gone to work for their uncle Cent, too, and had become an art dealer.

Theo, Vincent's brother

Vincent wrote to Theo and asked him for help. In his letter, Vincent said he felt trapped, as though he were in a "very dreadful cage."

Vincent wrote many letters to Theo. They often included drawings.

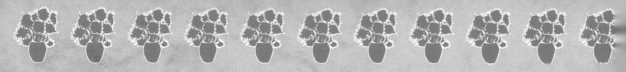

Theo encouraged Vincent and gave him money. Vincent began to work on his first real drawings and paintings. He wasn't always happy, but he kept working and learning. His work became better and better. In 1885, while living in the Dutch city of Nuenen, Vincent painted *The Potato Eaters*. He was very pleased with the painting.

When Vincent was thirty-three, he moved to Paris to live with Theo and paint. Many of the most talented artists of the time lived in Paris, and Vincent learned a great deal from them.

The Potato Eaters

(Right) Vincent painted this picture of himself in Paris.

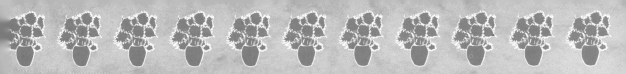

13

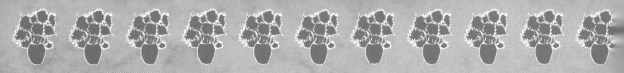

After two years, Vincent left Paris and went to Arles, a town in the south of France. He wanted to be near the sea, where the light was good and he could paint different types of pictures. It was 1888. Over the next sixteen months, he painted many of his most famous pictures.

Vincent painted this picture of his bedroom when he lived in Arles.

(Below) Arles is on the Rhône River.

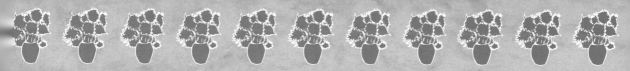

Vincent was a stranger in Arles. He had few friends. He asked the artist Paul Gauguin to visit him. One night, the two men had an argument. Later that night, Vincent cut off a piece of his left ear.

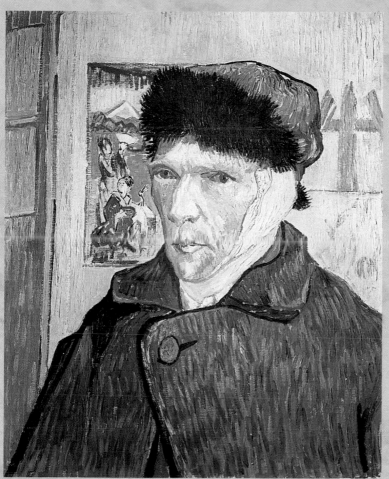

Vincent painted this picture of himself after cutting off part of his ear.

Vincent was fighting a mental illness. He had bad dreams and was often very depressed. He went into the hospital many times, but the doctors could not help him.

Although he was very sick, Vincent continued to paint. He even painted while he was in the hospital. His pictures were full of bright, swirling colors painted with bold brushstrokes.

Vincent painted several pictures of this café in Arles.

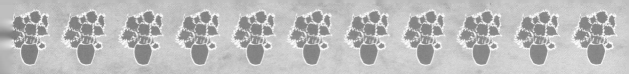

He painted pictures of the countryside and its trees and flowers. He painted pictures of the people he met and of ordinary objects, like chairs. He worked very quickly.

Starry Night has a big, swirling sky.

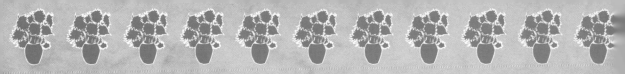

In May 1890, Vincent moved to the town of Auvers, near Paris. In the next two months, he painted many pictures, but he was still very sick.

Vincent was afraid he would never recover from his mental illness. One Sunday in July, he went for a walk in the countryside and shot himself.

The doctors could not save Vincent. Two days later, he died. He was thirty-seven years old.

Church at Auvers, one of Vincent's last paintings

(Right) Vincent liked to paint pictures of ordinary things, like his chair.

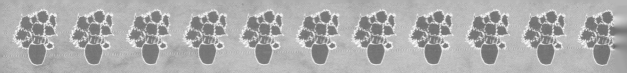

Vincent van Gogh died a poor man. He sold only one of his paintings during his lifetime. But more than a hundred years after his death, van Gogh's paintings are worth millions of dollars and he is one of the world's most beloved artists.

This painting of sunflowers is probably Vincent's most famous work.

Important Dates

1853 Vincent van Gogh was born

1857 Brother Theo born

1869 Began to work for uncle, an art dealer

1873 Sent to work in London

1874 Sent to work in Paris

1876 Returned to England to teach

1877 Went to Amsterdam to study religion

1878 Worked as minister in Belgium

1880 Decided to become artist

1885 Painted *The Potato Eaters*

1886 Moved to Paris

1888 Moved to Arles

1889 Entered hospital for long stay

1890 Moved to Auvers

Vincent van Gogh died

Vincent's early drawings show the flat land of the Netherlands.

21

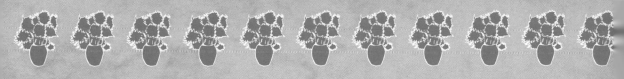

Key Words

art dealer
a person who buys and sells art

artist
a person who creates art

gallery
a place where art is displayed and sold

Index

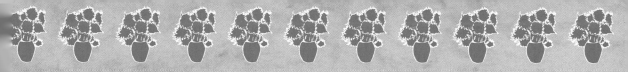

Acknowledgments

The author and publisher gratefully acknowledge the following for permission to reproduce copyrighted material:

Cover *Irises,* painted by van Gogh in 1889
J. Paul Getty Museum, Malibu, California/Bridgeman Art Library
Title page *Sunflowers* painted by van Gogh in 1888
Neue Pinakothek, Munich/AKG Photo
page 5 Rijksmuseum Vincent van Gogh, Amsterdam/Bridgeman Art Library
page 6 Vanderharst/Robert Harding Picture Library **page 7** (top) Rijksmuseum
Vincent van Gogh Amsterdam/AKG Photo (bottom) Rijksmuseum Vincent van
Gogh, Amsterdam/Bridgeman Art Library **page 8** (top) Rijksmuseum Vincent van
Gogh Amsterdam/AKG Photo (bottom) Hulton Deutsch **page 9** Kent County
Council Arts and Libraries **page 10** Kroller Muller Museum, Otterlo, The
Netherlands **page 11** (top right) Rijksmuseum Vincent van Gogh, Amsterdam/
AKG Photo (bottom left) Rijksmuseum Vincent van Gogh, Amsterdam/Bridgeman
Art Library **page 12** Rijksmuseum Kroller Muller, Otterlo/AKG/Erich Lessing
page 13 Francis G. Mayer/Corbis **page 14** (top) Musee D'Orsay, Paris/AKG/Erich
Lessing (bottom) T. D. Winter/Robert Harding Picture Library **page 15** Courtauld
Institute Galleries, University of London/Bridgeman Art Library **page 16**
Collection Hahnloser/AKG Photo **page 17** Museum of Modern Art, New
York/AKG Photo **page 18** Giraudon/Bridgeman Art Library **page 19** Tate Gallery,
London/ Bridgeman Art Library **page 20** Neue Pinakothek, Munich/AKG Photo
page 21 Noortman (London) Ltd/Bridgeman Art Library

About the Author

John Malam has a degree in ancient history and archeology from the University of Birmingham in England. He is the author of many children's books on topics that include history, natural history, natural science, and biography. Before becoming a writer and editor, he directed archeological excavations. Malam lives in Manchester, England, with his wife, Hilary, and their children, Joseph and Eve.